Lilah's Story

LIFE, LOVE AND LEGACY

Lilah Marshall

Published by Expert Message Group, LLC

Expert Message Group, LLC
P.O. Box 949
Tulsa, OK 74101

415.523.0404

www.expertmessagegroup.com

First Printing, April 2012

Copyright © Lilah Marshall, 2012
All Rights Reserved.

ISBN 978-1-936875-05-4

Printed in the United States of America
Set in Minion 13/19

Without limiting the rights under copyright reserved above, no part of this publication may be reproduced, stored in or introduced into a retrieval system, or transmitted, in any form, or by any means (electronic, mechanical, photocopying, recording, or otherwise), without the prior written permission of both the copyright owner and the above publisher of this book.

For permissions, please contact:

Expert Message Group, LLC
P.O. Box 949
Tulsa, OK 74101

Introduction

The secret to any pie recipe worth making is the little something sour in among all that sweet. It might sound like madness to you if you're not much of a baker, but I know a thing or two about pie — I'm a Bama lady, after all. You can take my word on this particular matter. Of course, you wouldn't know there's vinegar hiding in sticky pecan filling, or that Granny Smith apples are the only ones worth peelin' for the American classic. And anyone who knows anything about pie knows that heavy sour cherries are the only kind to use if you want people to come back for seconds. Yes, the secret to pie is unexpected but perhaps not so surprising: a little something tart to set off all that sugar.

Life is kind of like that.

What I mean, of course, is that we only really appreciate sunshine because we know what it's like to wake up to a rainy, overcast sky. We know how to embrace moments of joy because we know a little sadness might be around the corner. We know a good slice of pie when there's balance to the sweet — like I said, a little something sour.

The girls want to know about my life.

They're good girls, Cristi, Jen and Colleen. My daughter's girls. They know a lot of our family's history, which is wrapped up in the grand story of the Bama Pie Company, of course; but they've asked me to recall the particular part I played in making the Marshalls what they are today.

Looking back on my life is just like slicing into one of Big Mother's famous pies. At first the thing looks perfect sitting under a glass dome, resting on a crisp, white doily with scalloped lace around the edge. Just like that, I look back on the whole history of being me, Lilah Belle Drake Marshall, and I can't imagine a better-looking life. I had it all: a childhood the likes of which you can only find today watching old movies, complete with sweet parents who loved each other and siblings I cared for dearly; an education; a love straight out of a fairy tale that led to marriage and three beautiful children; and work to keep my hands busy and mind sharp. There the memories sit, protected in my mind, pristine and lovely.

A slice of Big Mother's pie might set you thinking of all the delicious pies you've had in the past. Maybe you think of spicy pumpkin pie around the Thanksgiving table, or plum pie at Christmas, or sky-high meringues at a greasy spoon along some highway where you stopped on a long road trip. Thinking about your life is just the same. You start with one memory and suddenly a whole chain of people and places start flashing through your mind.

After the cutting — that's when decisions need to be made. Do you tuck in head-on, eating the pointed end first and working toward the crust? Do you scoop out a bite from the middle, attacking the thing willy-nilly till it's gone? Are you the kind of person who starts at the crust and inches forward, savoring the filling only after you taste the buttery flake? You could say it doesn't matter — that any way you slice and eat it, pie is just pie. But we're working on the premise that pie is like life, remember? So how do I go about the business of savoring my memories? Do I start at the beginning — probably longer ago than you think — and move through time chronologically? Jump in at the middle like some Greek tragedy? Or start here, today, in the house Paul and I bought on Twenty-First Street in Oklahoma, and slowly make my way back to the Drake homestead in Capitol Hill?

Sure, sure, any way you go about it yields the same result; eating pie is eating pie is eating pie, and my story doesn't change based on when or where I start the telling. I suppose I'm only thinking about the matter at all because, as I said, I know a thing or two about pie. I know the weights and measures of the ingredients, the difference that room-temperature eggs make to the dough, how to keep crusts from cracking when you roll them to the right thickness… and I know about the sour in the sweet.

I suppose there are only two ways to help you see what I mean: jump into the telling of the story of my life, or have you swing on by the house for a piece of homemade pie. Of course you're welcome any time, but until then…

Chapter One

People say you come into this world alone and leave it alone, but those people probably weren't born to families with the twinning gene. It's hard to say now who's responsible — my Daddy's side, the Drakes, or Momma's people, the Burtons — but one of them had something extra that made us Drake kids come out in twos. My older sister, Velma, was exempted, but her daughters weren't. I had two brothers — Ross and Randall — who weren't twins but looked so much alike they might as well have been, and a twin sister all my own, Lelah Bernice. You can see Momma liked our names to match up, though I can't say if that was a matter of convenience or her personal preference. What I do know is that my middle name was taken from a certain Miss Belle who taught Momma her letters. That should give you an idea straightaway of how us Drake girls were meant to feel about getting our educations.

Lelah and I were as inseparable as could be. We spent our days playing jacks and tumbling down the big grassy hill where our house stood. There were two neighbor girls across the street we'd play with some, and the four of us would walk to the Lee School and back five days a week. Each day one of us would take a turn picking a song to sing on the way there, and we'd goof each other crooning like Louis Armstrong in "Muskrat Ramble" or imitating Gene Austin's particular whine in "Five Foot Two, Eyes of Blue." Every morning we'd walk through town with a song in our hearts and a skip in our steps — just the four of us girls.

Being twins, Lelah and I often found ourselves dressed alike, as was Momma's preference. She'd generally make all our clothes, though the boys were treated to store-bought pants and we got new church clothes at Easter. Our daily costume included black canvas Mary Janes and a cotton shift under a boxy, short-sleeved dress that fell about our knees. In the cooler months we'd add wool cardigans and long johns to the equation — and thanks to Santa's generosity one year, smart wool berets.

The Lee School was a big red brick affair with a blonde brick archway around the heavy wooden front door. I couldn't tell you if it was a remarkable place in any respect — geographically or educationally or whatnot — but it was where we learned our letters and numbers, and I don't remember it being particularly hard. Lelah and I didn't have time for extracurricular activities like the neighbor girls, though; no, at two in the afternoon we'd pack up our lunch pails and books and start the walk home on our own.

Eventually one of us would veer off to Daddy's office while the other one went home to help Momma with the house. We'd take turns, Lelah and me — playing secretary and playing house, that's what we'd say. "Whose week is it to play secretary?" I'd ask her on Sunday afternoons. "That'd be me, Lilah," she'd say, or vice versa. See, Daddy thought it was important that his girls knew all there was to know about working in the world, and that meant helping in his real estate business as well as learning to keep a home. No matter what life brought us, he reasoned, there would always be some kind of work for people who knew how to do it. So we learned cooking and cleaning and tending children with Momma, and answering the telephone, filing papers, and counting money with Daddy.

At the time in question, Oklahoma City and Capitol Hill were up-and-coming towns. Industry in Tulsa started growin' the city from the center outward, and soon enough workers and their families were sprawling all across the state. Black gold was the driving force behind all that city activity; Tulsa billed itself as the oil capital of the world, and as I understood it, we had enough there to supply the farthest reaches of the country.

Anyway, all those refinery workers and transportation folk and rich petroleum dealers needed places to stay — and that's where Daddy came in. Daddy Drake hailed from Tennessee, though beyond that I couldn't tell you much about how he found his way to Oklahoma. But he was there with his brother Jim who, for better or worse, was the more ambitious of the two. Daddy was really just concerned with gettin' people into a house that'd make 'em happy — he said his duty was to help people find their way home. Jim had his eye on the bottom line. Between the two of them, they made a pretty okay business. Daddy and Uncle Jim would buy old houses or empty lots and either fix up what was there or build something from scratch. Sometimes, if there were a lot of homes to build, we'd even stay in the houses while they went up. It was easier that way — all of us together under one roof instead of Daddy having to stay by himself while the building happened. It was good for us kids to see all the work that went into putting a roof over our heads, too, and of course that was one more kind of work Daddy said we ought to at least observe.

Daddy Drake was far from a real estate mogul, however. No, there were no Donald Trump characters in Oklahoma in the 1920s — not unless you count oil tycoons. Daddy did what he could in the business with Jim, Lelah and I helped where we could, and Momma did her bit and then some by keeping house and working part-time in the overall factory.

Even with all the work they did, Momma and Daddy were the sweetest couple. They were so good to each other — always polite, always "Yes, please" and "No, Paw" and "Yes, Maw" to one another. They showed us by example what a good partnership should look like. They were good people, our folks — good and honest and sweet as honey.

We were a God-fearing family — or God-loving, I should say. We went down to our church on Robinson Avenue every Sunday, just like all the other families in Capitol Hill. Robinson was called the "Avenue of Churches" because so many lined the street, and ours stood up with the best of 'em. We went to what you'd call a non-denominational church, the First Christian Church. It wasn't terribly popular — I suppose because they were strict. Stricter than regular churches.

Daddy always served as a deacon or an elder, and us kids would sit in the row with Momma, takin' extra care to control our pride when Daddy would get honored with a part in the service. Afterward we'd have to wait while a whole bunch of strangers shook his hand, but it never bothered us a lick. We were proud of our Daddy — and prouder still that we had the great responsibility of washing all the ceremonial wine cups after every service. There were two big, heavy silver cups to wash. Lelah and I would each carry one — the same one every week, she hers and me mine — admonishing each other the whole trip home not to drop it, not to drop it. 'Course had we dropped them, nothing would have happened. They were silver after all. But we always shared a big sigh when we crossed into the kitchen and put those precious cups on the table where they belonged. Out came the rags and a tin of polish Momma kept on a high shelf (away from Ross and Randall, who were like to use it as war paint). Lelah and I would buff those cups till we could see our faces staring back at us. Momma would inspect our work with a small nod; Daddy might tussle our hair. "Why, the Holy Spirit Himself would be pleased to drink his wine from one of these," he'd joke. We laughed every time.

Now as I said, me and Lelah were peas and carrots, and you could say our neighbors were a complement to our kinship, like mashed potatoes. But of course we had an older sister, Velma, who never seemed to make it to our picnics. See the thing is, Velma came along way back in 1906, ten years before me and Lelah. The truth is — and you couldn't have gotten Momma to admit it back when we were small, but she told me eventually — Lelah and me were something of a hiccough. Momma wouldn't use the word "accident" per se — no child of God is a mistake — but we weren't exactly part of her and Daddy's plans, either. Velma helped Momma raise us, there's no doubt about that, but by the time we were old enough to know what was going on, Velma was already up and gone. She married a young man by the name of Brock, but that's about all I have to say on the matter. The two of them divorced soon after the twins, Ramona and Naomi, were born. I don't recall Momma or Daddy ever saying much about Velma's husband or the divorce or anything like that. I only know that one of Momma's sisters helped Velma look after her little ones while she put herself through beauty school.

No, we weren't terribly close to Velma, and our relationship wasn't helped any when she came looking to practice some of what she'd learned in her program.

I remember the day clear as crystal. Velma came up the hill. Me and Lelah could see her from the upstairs bedroom where we were playing jacks. Lelah was winning — she was so fast at jacks — but I saw Velma out the window first. She had a big bag swinging down by her side. We ran down to meet her, curious about that bag. Out of it she pulled more gadgets and bottles than we'd ever seen. She told us she'd be giving us the newest look, a permanent curl. My hair was stick-straight, but I'd seen the curl Carole Lombard wore and I figured if it was good enough for her, it'd be plenty good for me.

Boy, was I wrong.

Velma did as good a job as I think anyone could do — sectioning our hair into what seemed like a hundred segments, twisting each around the curlers that stuck out of our heads at odd angles, steaming and applying the chemicals and all that. But when all was said and done, Lelah had lovely curls and I had a mop of frizz that was darn far from what I imagined topped the precious head of Carole Lombard.

Daddy's parents lived in Tulsa — the big city as far as I was concerned. They were quite a pair, Pappy and Mammy Drake: he was roly-poly and short where she was lithe and tall. They were always making us laugh and treating us to sweets. On weekends we'd all pile into a touring car Daddy borrowed, or onto the back of a horse-drawn flatbed, and head into Tulsa for a visit. Pappy and Mammy Drake would be ready for us with a picnic basket so big, me and Lelah could've used it as a boat. We'd all walk down to the Arkansas River and stake our claim on a spot of green. After lunch Pappy or Daddy would read to us from the Bible during our digestion; then off came our shoes, up hitched our skirts, and into the muddy waters we waded. On the walk back to Pappy and Mammy's — which always seemed particularly long once us kids were good and tuckered — Pappy would buy a paper cone filled with roasted pecans dusted in warm sugar and cinnamon. Those were the sweetest days I knew.

Sunday mornings were for church, naturally. We'd pile into whatever vehicle we came in and head back to Capitol Hill. We'd sing hymnals to the wide, flat landscape that seemed to stretch away from the road straight to infinity. Us kids would take turns reading from whatever Bible passage the preacher had discussed earlier in the day, and sometimes Daddy would test our memories about who begat whom, or who married whom, or who begat whom after marrying whomever. But the memory that's stayed with me most vividly after all these years is the image of my mother, sitting tall on the bench at the head of the hay-strewn wagon, late-afternoon sunlight making her dark hair glisten like wet leaves. She was a beautiful woman, my mother — strong and lovely and quick to laugh. She'd sway every so slightly where she sat, like she was always hearing music from somewhere far away. If I close my eyes and let myself drift back to the bed of a rocking wagon, let myself feel the sun baking my legs and face, let myself smell the dust… when I close my eyes and allow myself all that, it almost feels like I'm home.

Chapter Two

When Lelah and I were ten years old, word started spreading around town that the annual free fair in Tulsa would soon be coming to an end. Not an end exactly — the fair would continue to go up each year — but the familiar, fifteen-acre field north of Archer Street and Lewis Avenue would be abandoned for a 240-acre plot some oilman donated to the cause. I suppose he really loved the fair.

Like everyone else, me and Lelah knew that once the fair moved across town, it wouldn't be free anymore. We decided to visit as many attractions as possible during the single day we had to spend wandering the grounds. We had to time it right, since the only chance we had to go was when we were visiting our grandparents. In the week leading up to our visit, we were never more obedient! Our schoolwork and chores were done in a timely fashion. We helped our mother with extra cleaning, and made sure Daddy's office was in tip-top shape. When at last we arrived in Tulsa, we had built up the final fair to something of almost supernatural significance.

Suddenly those long rows of fancy cars on display seemed imbued with new importance; the small black bear cycling around on a painted white cart was all the more precious; harness racing was the most compelling sport we'd ever witnessed.

That year we rode each ride at least twice, some three times. We started the morning with the Tunnel Railway — refitted that year, we were told, to "emulate scenic Ireland" — then progress to its more spirited sister attraction, the Razzle Dazzle. Next we'd move along to the older electric rides, like the Chair-o-Plane and the Caterpillar, before breaking for lunch, which Momma always packed for us in a knapsack. We fulfilled our vow to Daddy to let our stomachs settle before hopping aboard the rides again. Instead we'd play ring toss and try to best each other knocking over weighted milk bottles. By the time the afternoon started its slow crawl toward dusk, we'd be ready for the main attraction: the Big Wheel.

Though it naturally dominated the fairground skyline, the Big Wheel was nestled in among the livestock tents and show rings at the center of the grounds. Now I can see the compulsion to force visitors through ring after ring of exhibitions to get to the main attraction, but back then it felt like the whole fair was conspiring to protect the Big Wheel from the outside world. Wending our way toward the center felt like moving through an enchanted forest, and enchanted we were. On the right kind of day, the boys in charge of loading the Wheel would let Lelah and me stay in our seat for two turns in a row — maybe even three. We'd swing our legs and squeal when our carriage rocked forward and back. Otherwise we'd just sit still, hands gripping the edge of the bench, eyes searching hungrily for the landmarks we knew so well on the ground. "There's our house!" one of us would call; but soon we'd find that the building in question couldn't have been our home. The world was transformed from up so high, and we were changed with it. When our feet once more stood on firm ground, something about the fair would lose its luster for the rest of the day and we'd head home. I suppose the same thing would happen to a grounded bird - who'd settle for walking after having tasted flight?

For as much as Momma and Daddy were hardy folk — we all were, it seemed, back then — Momma was never what one would consider a well woman. It was mostly her stomach that troubled her, though occasionally she'd have spells of exhaustion that no amount of sleep could tame. One year, Daddy told us kids we'd be taking a trip to Sulphur Springs for Momma to soak in the waters. Even though we knew Momma must have been feeling pretty awful for her to leave the overall factory and Daddy to leave the business for a full week, we were excited to camp out in a place we'd never been.

That is, of course, until we smelled the place.

Like the name suggests, Sulphur Springs is rife with pools fed underground through fissures in the earth. Sure, the water gets heated to a beautiful temperature on its way through those cracks, but by golly if it doesn't smell like rotten eggs. Lelah and I made a big show of wrinkling our noses and tying kerchiefs around our faces, even after we'd gotten accustomed to the aroma. We were mortified when Momma up and *drank* the foul-smelling water, but Daddy chided us for so obviously showing our distaste at a thing that could help our mother feel all right.

Naturally the smell of Sulphur Springs stands out in my mind as the most distinctive part of our first family vacation. But I also remember the squish of mud between my toes as my siblings and

I waded for minnows and frogs. I remember listening for cougars and bears at night — though Daddy assured me there were no such creatures around — and I especially remember the charred-over taste all our meals had from being cooked on an open fire. There were other families camping around us, and though I can't seem to recall with much clarity the names or faces of the children we played with, I know we all felt thick as thieves during our stay. In the evenings we'd hear the strains of a banjo from somewhere near the water, and of course Daddy or Momma would read to us from the Bible before bed.

Momma and Daddy would oblige us by folding back the canvas flaps of our tent when it was time for us to go to sleep, so my sister and I could count the stars as we drifted off. The two of them would stay up around the fire, the hum and lilt of their voices mingling with the orchestra of crickets and cicadas. I remember fighting the urge to sleep, the sensation that I'd miss out on something wonderful if I closed my eyes making me something close to anxious. Each morning the sunlight peeking through the slits of the tent would urge me awake with its bright, easy persistence.

For folks like us, accustomed to working every day, it was a precious time. I don't know that the water did Momma any good, but just getting away from our familiar routine seemed to rejuvenate her some. She was such a good woman, my Momma — and it was hard to see her bear the burden of an infirm body. But bear it she did, and without complaint. If only her lot had been easier.

It was on our way home from Sulphur Springs that us Drake kids got our first glimpse of what real tragedy was. Daddy had borrowed a touring car from one of his real estate contacts, as he often did for our trips to visit Pappy and Mammy Drake. This particular time, he managed to procure a 1929 Packard DeLuxe. The top was busted. Daddy explained how, but I wasn't really listening on account of checking my reflection in the smooth gloss on the hood. The Packard's long nose extended out from a two-row cab that could comfortably seat six, but all our camping equipment amounted to a seventh and eighth person. Ross and Randall vied for spots facing backward on the rumble seat, their bottoms bouncing precariously on the rear edge of the back seat. Lelah and me were happy to sit up front with Daddy, of course, and Momma snuggled in the back next to all our things.

That was all on the way *to* Sulphur Springs. On the way home, we'd exhausted a lot of our supplies and most of Momma's patience. When Ross and Randall starting roughhousing over who'd get to sit where, she settled the matter once and for all by taking over the rumble seat and letting them figure out how to arrange themselves inside the cab. Things got a bit quiet after that — us girls were naturally suppressing our giggles — until the tense silence was broken by a heavy thud and sharp cry from behind us. "Momma!" Ross screamed before he seemed to choke on his own voice. Daddy was out of the car before I knew what was happening, but it sure didn't take long for us to figure it out. The busted roof canvas had torn at the seam where Momma had been holding on, and she rolled right off the back bumper into the road. We were all shaken up — Momma especially, of course — but she wasn't hurt at all. As a family, though, we'd never been so close to knowing the kind of heartache that breaks people in two.

Lelah and I were inconsolable. We kept feeding each other what-ifs, each one more horrific than the last. What if Momma had slipped under a wheel? What if one of her legs had gotten stuck and she'd been dragged along? What if we'd lost the most precious gem God had seen fit to put down smack in the heart of Oklahoma?

Though it was she who fell, Momma was the one who ended up soothing us. Ross and Randall squeezed up front with Daddy and us girls flanked our Momma, hugging her so hard around the middle that I wasn't sure where Lelah's arms ended and mine began. We stayed just that way the whole ride home.

By the time Lelah and I got past the Lee School and into Capitol Hill High, we were well accustomed to the routine of our lives: school in the mornings and into the afternoon, helping Momma and Daddy from the afternoon into the evening, homework before and after supper, in bed by nine. If it sounds like we had a simple life, that's because we did. Mind, I didn't say it was an easy life — few people had it easy during a time history has come to remember as the Dust Bowl — but there was a certain clarity around our lives that I've watched the world lose as I've lived in it.

Capitol Hill High may not have had row upon row of computers back then — heck, we didn't even have row upon row of typewriters — but it was where we went to expand our horizons past the flat expanse of Oklahoma. I liked history and English best, while Lelah excelled at math. Sometimes we'd find ourselves in a tiff trying to explain our favored subjects to one another, but eventually we just figured that even for twins some things couldn't get split evenly down the middle. There were enough brains to go around, but not so much that we could both be good at everything. We had plenty of pretty, though. At least, that's what Momma said.

Though the bulk of our lives was spent in school and at work, we found time to play, too. The thirties were a glorious time for the silver screen: Charlie Chaplin, Mae West, Shirley Temple, and the Marx brothers all made their way to the single-screen theatre across the river. Once a month Lelah and me and our girlfriends would head to a picture, even if it was one we'd already seen. Lelah liked the scary stuff — Dracula and Frankenstein and the like. I nurtured a soft spot for the song and dance routines in Shirley Temple's films. She had an innocence I liked that made me feel grown-up.

There were so many churches in Capitol Hill, we could count on at least one of them sponsoring a dance each week. Pews would get pushed to the edges of the sanctuary and a rough platform that always seemed on the verge of collapse would find its way in front of the altar. A band would set up, and us girls would get all dolled up to go Charleston and tango and shimmy the night away. Some of the gals even learned to swing, though that was a bit ambitious for me and my friends. The thing was, swing required a swingee and a swinger — and the latter we didn't have.

Lelah and I weren't interested in dating. The truth is, we didn't have time. There were a few handsome young men we knew from church and school, but we could never accept invitations to cheer at football games after school or take long drives on Saturday afternoons. We both had obligations to Momma and Daddy, and our time on the weekends was largely consumed by family obligations and time at church. The dance hall was the one place we could have done some flirting, but it never really occurred to us.

Chapter Three

Even though Lelah and I were both familiar with real estate thanks to Daddy, we both set off on our own to find work outside the family business after graduating from Capitol Hill High. There weren't so many employment options in our part of the state at the time, especially for two young ladies like us. Agricultural work had been on the decline for a decade, and the drought that had moved into the region in 1930 didn't seem to want to break. Nearly half the workers in the city were unemployed, and income from farming dwindled to nearly nothing. The newspaper trumpeted the statistics: 300,000 OUT OF WORK — POPULATION DWINDLES AS DROUGHT DRAGS ON. Times were hard to say the very least, but Lelah and I knew we had to find a way to earn our living.

When we were growing up, my sister and I naturally thought we'd end up working in one of the automobile factories — Midland Motor or the Ford plant — or even in one of the aircraft manufacturing plants in town. Lelah and I imagined ourselves working the phones or helping keep books, maybe even starting out somewhere on the line. We weren't afraid to get our hands dirty. Trouble was, plants started closing during the winter of 1932, and the doors hadn't reopened by the time we were ready to work.

Momma and Daddy were the ones who gave me the idea to start thinking a little outside the box. "People still have to eat," Momma said one day over supper. "They do indeed," Daddy added, "and they especially have to eat what they can't cook themselves." The next morning, my first stop was Colonial Bakery on Northwest Eighteenth Street. I still remembered the advertisement for Colonial that had run in the papers a handful of years earlier: "Oklahoma's most modern bakery." I didn't quite know what that meant, but there was one aspect of Colonial's operation that needed no explanation: each day, rows of white-uniformed men and women filed in the single door at the center of the grey cement factory, and each evening they knocked off around four o' clock in the afternoon to head home. The people there looked happy to show up each day, and why not? They worked in a place that smelled delicious all day long, and I figured they got some tasty treats as part of their pay, too. At a time when so many in the country didn't remember what it was like not to be hungry, that counted for a lot.

I'm not sure why I was surprised to find out that Colonial wasn't hiring, but I took it as a tough blow. Of course no one would leave a job like that, I told myself. I knew I had to buck up and try something new. My next stop was the Griffin Grocery Company, famous for all sorts of tasty items: syrups, baking products, jelly, preserves, mustard, peanut butter, and Ross and Randall's favorite Sunday morning breakfast accessory, Griffin's Waffle Syrup. I fancied myself quite practical for thinking to get a position at a company that made things we needed around the house. Of course, I didn't realize at the time that working for a place didn't make you entitled to have any of what you worked so hard to produce — not necessarily, anyway. But I guess that lesson came later. Then, I was still learning that wanting a job didn't always mean finding one. Griffin's Grocery made that abundantly clear, and the discouragement I felt reached new lows.

I was sharing my consternation with Momma and Daddy that night over another family supper. We were lucky to have food, our house, and clothes on our backs. I knew that, but I wanted to do my part. Lelah wasn't having much luck either, so at least I had some company in my desperation.

"It'll all work out, Lilah," Momma said. "It always does. But until then, have a little pie and don't forget to say your prayers." I didn't know it just then, but I'd soon find out: pies and prayers were about to have a lot to do with one another for Lilah Drake.

Chapter Four

"Have you ever made a pie?"

"Yes, ma'am, I have."

"And have you ever had a Bama Pie?"

"Yes, ma'am. Just the other night, in fact. It was pecan. And delicious, I might add."

The woman sitting across from me smiled a warm smile that showed off her pretty white teeth. Flour clung to the hair on her arms and the contrast made her look tan, even though I knew she must work inside the factory all day and not see too much sun.

"I like the pecan, too," she said.

That afternoon, Grace introduced me to Melvin, her husband, with whom she ran the Oklahoma City branch of the Bama Pie Company. Bama had started in Dallas in 1927, she explained, founded by Henry and Alabama Marshall, her parents. Alabama — or "Big Mother" as the family called her — had been working in Woolworth's at the luncheonette counter. She worked her way up, and soon she was in charge of making all the pies for Woolworth's, and soon enough the store had to expand its counter to make room for all the people clamoring to eat Big Mother's pies. When Henry got wind of what was going on, he convinced his wife to stop working at Woolworth's and put her pie-making skills to good use for the family. They started Bama Pie out of their home kitchen and, with the whole family helping, grew the business into something of an enterprise. Now they were expanding by opening pie plants around the Midwest, and it just so happened the Oklahoma City branch was in need of an extra set of hands.

I was hired to scour pots and mix dough, learn the Bama family recipes, and weigh out the ingredients for all the fillings. I was also hired to clean Grace's house every third Saturday of the month. It was good work, although hard at first, like all new things. The first day was the hardest, in no small part because I decided to show up wearing the shoes I thought would make me look most adult: a pair of black leather Mary Jane pumps. Prior to that day, I'd only ever worn those for dances or church — and I'd certainly never stood in them for hours and hours on end. By the time I got home that night, my dogs were barkin' something awful. Momma told me to lie down on the couch before dinner and she'd call me when it was time. I dozed off right away, and woke up to the sounds and smells of dinner making its way to the table. Well, I was famished. I'd just put in my first full day of work at my first real job, after all. I swung my legs over the side of the couch and pushed myself upright… and couldn't take a single step. My feet were so swollen and sore, I had to prop them up again just to keep the blood from rushing into my soles too fast. Sweet Momma let me eat where I lay, but I learned my lesson all the same. The next day and every one thereafter, I was in flats.

I learned a lot from Grace, and I like to think I was an apt pupil. Miniature pecan pie shells were my specialty. I couldn't even begin to guess how many of those little rounds I made. The shop was open six days a week, of which I generally worked five. As I mentioned, though, on the third Saturday of each month I'd come in to clean the house, which was attached to the back of the shop. I enjoyed my time making pies, but I surprised myself by taking a real shine to cleaning Grace and Melvin's place, too. I liked the easy solitude I felt moving from room to room, systematically working from surface to surface with a duster and polish. I also liked feeling as if I was getting to know Grace and Melvin. They'd been so kind to me, and I so enjoyed working with them in the shop, that being in their private home seemed a privilege.

I was particularly fond of my work in the living room, as that's where Grace had hung all her family photos. There was one of Bama and Henry sitting in two wingchairs positioned on a front lawn. They looked dressed for church or a wedding, and Bama had her hands and ankles crossed daintily. Henry was on her right in a just-slightly-too-big suit and a tie. It was hard not to smile back at that photo, so usually I did.

There was another picture in a gilded wooden frame — a candid from Grace's youth. In it, she stood in the foreground in a light-colored dress and dark shoes, her arms thrown casually over the shoulders of a slightly shorter woman whose identity I never really bothered to learn. The girls were looking in opposite directions as if so much was happening outside the frame, they couldn't take it all in at once. Behind them, faces shadowed, were a young boy on a bicycle and a man in a vest and tie. Both seemed to be taking pains to stay out of the shot, but neither was totally successful. That picture reminded me of the Drake homestead, always bustling with activity and maybe a touch of chaos.

There were lots of pictures in that room. I used to know the exact number, and considering how often I picked up each frame, dusted it, returned it to its place, and adjusted it to hang properly, I guess that's no surprise. One photo in particular, though, struck me a little more profoundly than the rest. Like a lot of Marshall family photos, this one took place next to a delivery truck. Bama trucks were a big part of the business, and bringing in a new one was usually cause for a little celebration — or at least a quick picture. Anyway, in this particular instance, a young man who seemed about my age had a foot propped on the runner of a gleaming black delivery truck. One hand was on his hip and the other rested casually on the edge of the roof. He had warm, light eyes and blondish hair parted on the left and slicked smooth to the right. I thought his ears were sweet — narrow at the bottom and a little broad at the tops — and his smile seemed to come easy.

Yes, I thought the boy in that picture was mighty handsome. Too handsome for a girl like me.

One morning, as I started up the mixers and began baking off apple pies for the afternoon deliveries, I heard a new voice coming from Grace and Melvin's quarters. I didn't think too much of it. It was no business of mine, after all. But when the three of them strolled into the shop I took a peek at the mystery man making Grace and Melvin laugh so hard so early in the day.

And who should I see standing there, easy smile and sweet ears and light eyes and all? Surely it couldn't have been — but it was. The boy from the picture had come to life, and I'd be lying if

I didn't say my first thought was that the camera hadn't done him a lick of justice.

Yes, that was the day Paul Marshall walked into my life — or rather, the day our lives finally converged at Bama Pie. It would be another few months before Paul finally asked me out, and another two months after that before he asked for my hand… but it all started that bright, cinnamon-scented morning.

Chapter Five

Even though we worked for the same small company, Paul and I didn't find many excuses to speak to one another in those first weeks. I learned through the grapevine that Paul had come up to visit Grace and Melvin after having a falling-out with his father down at the original Bama plant. He'd come to Oklahoma City to keep his mind in the business while getting some distance from his daddy. It wasn't long before the opportunity to take over a route came up, and after that it seemed Paul had been with us all along.

Paul was handsome — so handsome I thought I'd never have a chance with him. Still, I let myself enjoy the anticipation of seeing him each day. Never does a woman feel so alive as when she's feeling the flutter of new love in her heart.

One day in mid-September of 1935, Grace sent me into town to pick up envelopes and other office supplies. The weather was monstrous that day. One of those late-summer soaking storms was dumping rain in buckets, and the roads were treacherous. I was a fairly confident driver, but even so, I could feel my car fishtailing every now and again. Getting into town took ages, and when I got there, I couldn't find anywhere to park near the post office. I was resigned to feeling wet and cold the rest of the day — I'd forgotten my umbrella — when through the gray rain I saw my saving grace: a Bama delivery truck! I pulled up right alongside the truck, whose driver must have popped into a store for a delivery, blocking the truck in so that if the driver were to come out, he would be stuck there. I prayed I wouldn't be holding anyone up too long as I dashed into the post office. Sure enough there was a line — you can always count on the world slowing down just as you're determined to speed it up — but I thought I'd done rather well when I ducked back into the car in under ten minutes. I checked my hair 'do in the mirror. "Ruined," I thought to myself, "but at least I can cover it with a cap at the shop." But before I could so much as attempt to smooth a particularly rebellious clump of frizz back into place, I was startled near out of my seat by someone abruptly opening the passenger-side door.

"Now, look here," a voice began. The figure looming in the doorway was headless until he ducked under the frame to shield himself from the downpour. "When you see a deliv—"

"Oh! Hello, Paul," I said.

"Oh. Hello, Lilah," said Paul.

"I hope you don't mind my parking like this," I said. "Grace sent me to buy some envelopes and stamps, but the traffic is so bad today there wasn't any place to park. I was so glad I saw a Bama truck parked here."

I could see how annoyed Paul was that I had blocked him in, and I hoped my embarrassment wouldn't show in the deep blush I felt creeping up my cheeks. To my great relief, Paul's features softened into the warm smile I'd come to know from his picture.

"Oh, that's all right," he said. "We Bama Pie people have to stick together."

"Well, I guess I'd better get out of your way. I know being one of the top route men means you need to keep moving. I'm sorry I slowed you down."

"It's all right," Paul said. There followed a long pause. I don't know what was going through Paul's mind at that moment, but my brain was a jumble of what felt like a thousand different thoughts. I was worried about looking a mess from the rain, still anxious that I'd upset Paul, and secretly thrilled that we'd run into each other away from the prying eyes of the plant. Even though we were in the most public place imaginable, this was still the most private moment we'd shared.

"I guess I'll go now," I offered. "But Paul? It was nice talking to you."

"Yes, and you, too," he said.

When Paul turned to go I could see his entire back was soaked through, and I felt even more awful than before! Part of me wished he'd yanked that door open and climbed right in next to me, even if it was to yell something fierce at me for having blocked him in. As I drove away, I imagined the two of us in the front seat, the rain pelting the roof and blocking out the rest of the world. It would have been nice.

After that, Paul started saying hello to me in the shop. At first his greetings were just nods of his head coupled with a tug on the front of his cap. But he worked up to "Mornin'" or "Hi, there," and eventually, "Hi, Lilah." Early mornings at the shop became my favorite part of each day; I'd be sure to arrive before Paul came to load his deliveries, and I collected those little greetings in my heart like a squirrel storing away nuts for the winter. Each one was precious.

In the middle of October that same year, everything changed.

It was a day like any other, except it happened to be Paul's twenty-first birthday. When he got back to the shop after making his deliveries, Grace hailed him with a "Happy Birthday" that triggered all of us to wish him our best — and of course I hoped with all my heart that he really would have an excellent year. When the hullabaloo had died down a bit, Melvin cleared his throat some and clapped Paul on the shoulder.

"Well, Paul," he said, "today you're a man, huh?"

"I guess so," Paul said.

"In that case, are you man enough now to ask Lilah for a date?"

I felt like all the air had been sucked out of the room at once. I was sure my face was cherry-filling red and hot to the touch, and I trained my eyes on what was suddenly a very interesting linoleum floor.

I was busy selecting a few choice words to share with Melvin later for having put me and Paul on the spot that way, when I heard Paul shuffle his feet and clear his throat.

"I guess I am," he said, his tone strained but confident. "How about it, Lilah?"

It was exactly the question I'd been waiting for, but it certainly wasn't asked the way I had hoped it would be. I kept my eyes lowered even though I could feel Paul and everyone else in the shop staring me down. "I don't know," I whispered.

"Maybe if you'd ask her in private, she'd be more cooperative, Paul," Melvin offered. *Hasn't that guy done enough today?* I thought.

Grace managed to get everyone to disperse and I escaped to the back room to scrub pots and scour pans. The other girls I worked with could see how shy I felt, so no one really said anything to me.

Later that night, while I was heading for the door, Paul fell in beside me.

"Lilah, I didn't mean to embarrass you today, but Melvin kind of got us both in a corner."

"I know you didn't mean anything, Paul," I said.

"I did mean what I said, actually," Paul answered, his voice full of intensity. "I do want to take you out. The reason Melvin said what he did is because I already told him that one day I was gonna ask you for a date. I just never got the nerve, so he forced the words outta me. I'm glad he did, too."

My heart was fluttering so quickly in my chest I thought it would fly right out of my mouth. "I'd be happy to go out with you, Paul."

"Okay then, it's a date."

"It's a date."

Lelah had been sewing a new frock since mid-June from a design she'd seen in McCall's style news, but she'd essentially missed the chance to wear it since work kept her from making too much headway. But when my sister found out I had a date with Paul Marshall, she did what any good twin would: she burned the midnight oil to finish the dress in time for my date.

The cut and color were lovely. Lelah had chosen a midnight-blue jersey for versatility's sake, but I couldn't have imagined a nicer fabric for all the world. The top was long-sleeved with an elbow-length cape effect accentuated by three neat bows along the mid-seam. A long skirt with three shallow pleats fell to mid-calf; I wore my good church shoes and a patent leather belt. Even though I saw Paul every day, I was nervous as anything about him showing up at our door to pick me up. I had to laugh at myself when he finally arrived. I was shocked to see him pull up in a 1930 Model A he'd borrowed from a friend; I realized I had expected to be taken out in one of the Bama trucks!

"Evening, Lilah," Paul said. "You sure look nice."

"You too, Paul. Nice to see you out of uniform."

Paul smiled. I knew he must appreciate seeing me out of the grey Bama uniform, too. Suddenly we were two kids with the world at our fingertips instead of two employees working hard every day to make ends meet.

"You ready to go?" Paul asked, opening the passenger-side door for me.

"I surely am," I said. *I'd go anywhere with you,* I thought.

Our first stop was Sully's Diner, one of the more popular places around for people our age. We sat in a corner booth and ordered burgers and Cokes. It was so easy to talk to Paul on that first date. All my nerves dissolved as we laughed and told stories about our families and school memories. Paul told me he'd left school after the 8th grade to help with the family business. Paul and his family had just moved from Dallas to Waco and back again.

"One day," Paul said, pausing to swallow a mouthful of burger, "I saw Mama and Dad leaving off to drive the Corsicana route. That was the longest route we had back then. I knew they wouldn't be home until late, and then they'd have to start off early in the morning again the next day and the next day and the day after that. I marched down the hallway to the school's main office and put my books on the counter. 'I'm Paul Marshall and these are my books. I'm going to work,' I told the woman there. And you know what?"

"What, Paul?"

"She just looked at me and smiled and said 'Good luck.'"

I nodded in silent understanding. Paul's story was one I'd heard before. Plenty of kids had left school during those lean years. People were forced to go wherever there was work, no matter how far it took them from all the things they knew and loved.

"Do you regret it, Paul?" I asked. I knew it was a bold question, but I had to know. Paul chewed thoughtfully before he answered.

"Do I regret having to leave school? Yes, I do. Us Marshalls like to finish what we start. So yes, I regret that part of what happened. But do I regret stepping up to the family business and contributing to Bama? Not in the least."

Paul's eyes sparkled with renewed intensity as he leaned in closer. "See, I've got big plans for Bama. I think we can increase production rates and decrease costs by harnessing new machines and baking techniques. I'd venture a guess that I can build up our routes significantly. Given enough time, of course."

Paul hinted that his willingness to embrace new technologies — automatic dough rollers and newly modeled industrial ovens — was part of what brought him up to Oklahoma City. See, Paul's dad disagreed with his son's assessment of the business and wanted to keep doing things the way they'd always been done. But while Paul had tried to leave the family business and strike out on his own time and again, he always ended up coming back to Bama. Pie was in his blood, he said, even when working with the family made that same blood boil. Ultimately he'd realized that the best way to serve Bama was by coming up to Grace and Melvin's shop.

"But coming up here has proved mighty good in more ways than one," Paul said.

"Oh? How's that, Paul?" I asked.

"Well I've taken over a route that wasn't doing well and turned it around, so that's one thing," Paul explained. "I've gotten to spend time with my sister and Melvin, so that's another. And..." Paul trailed off and reached for his Coke, but found it empty. He rubbed his hands together, smoothed back the hair by his right temple, then folded and re-folded his napkin on his lap.

"Paul?" I asked, "Is everything okay?"

"What I was going to say," he said, his voice softer now, "was that coming up here has proved mighty good in more ways than one. And the one most outstanding way is that here, I met you."

Sully's faded away around us until Paul and I were the only two people in the room. I surrendered myself to those sweet blue eyes and felt something pass between us that I don't think I can ever really put into words. Looking back on that moment from the vantage point of many years of experience, I can only describe it as the moment I knew my life would never be the same: it was the moment I fell in love.

Like lights coming up in a theatre after a picture show, the scene slowly materialized around us until we were once again two kids in a corner booth at an old diner in Oklahoma. We finished our burgers and Paul treated — "Don't even think about it," he said. I was a little sad that the night had to end so soon.

"You're not too tired, are you, Lilah?" Paul asked once we got in the car. "I know you put in a long week just like the rest of us."

"Why, that's very sweet of you, Paul, but no, I'm not tired."

"Well, good," said Paul, and I saw that mischievous sparkle twinkling in his eyes again. "Because I thought I'd take you for a little spin."

And spin we did, at a little roller rink behind one of the churches in town. Paul had borrowed a set of skates for me and vowed he wouldn't let me fall. I was a rather good skater, in fact, but Paul certainly didn't know that and I wasn't about to tell him. I let him take my hand and lead me out to the rink wall, let him show me how to push off my back foot and glide forward on the front. I held on tight to his offered arm — for stability, of course — and soon enough we were having a grand old time making steady circles around the rink.

When we were good and tuckered, we sat on an old wooden bench sipping hot chocolates Paul had gotten from the little stand near the rink. I'd come to learn that Paul was great that way — he always knew where to get exactly what we needed, exactly when we needed it. We stayed glued to that bench for hours, trading stories and anecdotes. It was like we couldn't wait to get each other caught up on everything that had happened to us in our lives prior to meeting. By the time Paul walked me to my front door, I felt like I had a new best friend.

"I sure had a nice time tonight, Lilah," Paul said.

"The best, Paul, really," I answered. I meant it, too.

"I hope you'll let me take you out again soon."

"I'd like that, Paul."

There was a long pause I wasn't sure how to fill, since I knew this moment was when a lot of boys would have tried for a first kiss. I hadn't told Paul that this was my first real date, but it was. Truth be told, I wasn't sure a kiss was the proper way to end it.

Paul took my hands in his and smoothed the backs of my palms with his thumbs in the most unexpected, gentle way.

"Until then," he said, slowly releasing his grasp.

"Until then."

Chapter Six

It wasn't two months later when Paul and I found ourselves in another café downtown called Erving's. We were discussing a topic that had become commonplace between us. In my mind, I had come to refer to these conversations as our "Dream Big Talks," because that's exactly what they were about.

Even though I had grown up not wanting for anything, I had still worked my whole life and knew the value of a dollar. Like Paul, I'd seen my neighbors struggle to find work during the Depression, seen good people go hungry, seen children grow thin and sallow at church while their parents withered beside them. It wasn't easy living where we did, when we did. Paul and I both knew that. We also knew we wanted better things for ourselves and our families in the future.

That's how Dream Big Talks came to be. I confided in Paul that I'd marched down to the bank and opened a savings account with my first paycheck from Grace. I could only afford to put five dollars in the account, but it was more money than I'd ever had in a bank.

Heck, it was the only money I'd ever had in a bank. Paul seemed impressed with me, and I glowed under his proud gaze. "Smart and beautiful," he said. "How'd I get so lucky?"

At Erving's, over a shared soda, Paul started in about striking out on his own.

"I want to have my own business one day," he said, and the urgency in his voice was somehow different than the usual intensity I had grown to love.

"I know, Paul. I've had those same feelings."

"I don't mean when I'm eighty. I mean now. I want to start it soon. I believe the pie business can really go places if it's handled right."

"I know that too, Paul. You'd be great as a business owner, and there's no business you know better than pie. You're the best route man Bama's got. And I know it might take a while to learn, but I don't mind doing the dirty work around the shop. I've been watching Grace all these months, and I think I could run a shop as well as she does."

"It's true. You could..." Paul trailed off. He seemed to be thinking hard about something.

"Lilah, you know I think you're about the most wonderful girl in the world," he said. "But I really want to start something. I mean really. Starting a business is no easy task. It's a lot of hard work and long hours. There's no money in any kind of business at the beginning, even a business that's attached to an established company like Bama. That means a man striking out on his own doesn't have much to offer someone... someone like a wife. Do you understand what I'm saying, Lilah?"

Time seemed to slow to a stop. Part of me couldn't believe what I was hearing, but another part of me understood: Paul had to pursue his dreams. His ambition was as much a part of him as his warmth or his smile or those bright blue eyes. It was part and parcel of what I'd grown to adore so much in the past months. I couldn't be angry that he felt having a steady like me was holding him back — but a part of me was more crestfallen and heartbroken than I'd ever thought possible. I blinked back hot tears that had sprung to the back of my eyes.

"I — I understand, Paul." A sob managed to escape my throat and I looked down at my lap before Paul could see me cry.

"Lilah? Lilah, what's the matter?" Paul asked, lifting my chin with a gentle hand. "If I'd known this was gonna upset you so much, I wouldn't have brought it up."

"You had to, Paul, I know you did. But you can't expect me not to be upset. I mean, I thought we were having a good time together… at least, I've been having a great time with you, Paul. I guess I just didn't see the end coming—"

"The end?"

"Well, sure, Paul, the end. I heard you. I know you have to strike out on your own without any distractions, and that's all I'd be, isn't it? A distraction? Paul? I don't think this is terribly funny, actually, so I'm not sure why you're smiling."

"Lilah, Lilah. You thought I was breaking things off with you so I could go into the pie business on my own?"

"Isn't that what you said?"

"What I said — what I was trying to say — is that the road I intend to travel won't be an easy one paved with gold bricks and silver spoons. It's the only road for me, though, and seeing as how I wouldn't want to walk it with anybody else… Lilah, I'm asking you to come with me. Be my wife. Will you marry me, Lilah?"

"Yes!" I answered. "Of course I will!"

DAILY BEACON SOCIETY PAGE

November 19, 1935

(by Marie Denry Luttrefl — Phone 3-2391)

Mr. and Mrs. David C. Drake, 312 SW Thirtieth St., today announced the engagement of their daughter, Miss Lilah Drake, to Paul Marshall, son of Mr. and Mrs. H.C. Marshall of Dallas, Texas. No definite date has been set for the ceremony, but tentative arrangements are being made for a post-holiday affair in late December. Miss Drake is a graduate of the Capitol Hill Senior High School. Mr. Marshall is associated with the Bama Pie Co., of the city.

The *Daily* had it almost right — we didn't quite wait until the holidays had passed. Paul and I got married on the Friday before Christmas — December twenty-third, 1935. It was a small ceremony, just family and a few close friends, but the joy of the day seemed to blend with the cheer inherent to Christmastime in the most extraordinary way. It was like we couldn't smile wide enough or laugh long enough to express the way we felt inside. We were simply bursting with our love for each other.

That was the first time Big Mother and Big Daddy met my family. At dinner they told the story of how they met. Big Daddy was a traveling salesman, selling vacuums door-to-door. At the time, folks in that business would rely on the kindness of their potential customers to put them up overnight. One night, Big Daddy found himself at Big Mother's house. "That was before I got to be known as 'Big Mother,'" Big Mother joked. We all laughed. Even to those who'd only known the Marshalls a short time, it was clear that Mother ruled the roost.

Yes, that year's Christmas was one of the sweetest I can remember. Paul and I were together, our families were joined for the first time, and the future was as fresh and full of promise as it could have been. Paul and I were determined to make the ideas we'd discussed during our Dream Big Talks a reality, and each week we agreed to put ten dollars aside. We both knew it would take a lot of money to strike out on our own, but we had our sights set on Tulsa. Aside from the fact that Tulsa was a growing community with lots of potential, the place appealed to us for more practical reasons: it was close enough to Oklahoma City and Dallas that we could count on extra support if we needed it. It was an untapped market to open a brand new branch of Bama – our own little pie shop.

Paul and I were focused and driven to succeed, but our plans were derailed, as plans often are. By the end of February 1936, we found out I was pregnant. We were overjoyed, of course, but our dreams of Tulsa would have to be put on hold.

Or so we thought.

Paul's brother, Bud, and his wife Ruth showed up to visit Grace and Melvin in early June. I was already sporting a belly by then, but I was dressed and ready to go when Paul came home from work. We hopped in the car and made our way to the miniature family reunion. It wasn't long after we arrived that all six of us were in stitches listening to the Marshall clan recount stories from their childhood. The more I got to know about Paul's family and the Bama company, the more it seemed like good humor was essential to the growth of both entities. Good humor and, of course, hard work.

"Did I ever tell you about how Daddy started Bama?" Paul asked me.

"I know about Mother's work at Woolworth's, and how Daddy encouraged her to bring all that good business home," I answered.

"Sure, that's how the idea of Bama started. But did I ever tell you about how we got to the nitty-gritty of making actual pies?"

"I don't believe you have," I said.

"How could you have let her join the family without telling her *that* story?" Grace asked.

"Well I don't rightly know, actually," said Paul, and again we found ourselves dissolving in giggles.

"Paul! Now you've got to tell me. I feel plain silly not knowing," I said.

"Okay, okay, but you have to promise not to run off scared when you realize how crazy us Marshalls are."

"Seeing as how I'm a Marshall now too, I solemnly swear it," I said.

"Thatta girl," he said with a wink. Rubbing his hands together, he continued.

"Once Daddy got it into his head that Mother's pies could make us some money of our own, he went about the difficult task of supplying his new business. 'I need all our money for supplies,' he told Mother. And with a weary look all us kids recognized too well, she handed it all over. All one-dollar-sixty-seven-cents of it. That might have stopped another man in his tracks, but you've met Daddy. You know nothing could ever really stop him once he's got an idea in his head.

"So Daddy took that dollar-sixty-seven and marched right down to Charles Dennery Bakery Supply. He introduced himself to the woman behind the counter as Mister H.C. Marshall, owner of the Bama Pie Company, and asked to speak with a manager. He was directed to Mr. Mooreland. 'Mr. Mooreland,' Daddy said, 'I've recently established the Bama Pie Company. Because of your company's high standards and impeccable reputation, I've chosen to purchase my supplies from you.'

"Mr. Mooreland, pleased as punch, grabbed a pencil and an order form and asked Daddy what he needed. 'One gallon of cherries, two gallons of apples, one gallon of pineapple, five pounds each of dried apples and peaches, two twelve-quart enamel pans, two dozen seven-inch pie pans and one pound each of salt and cinnamon.' Mr. Mooreland wrote everything down and sent a stock boy to load up our car. 'That'll be twenty-five dollars and fifty cents, Mr. Marshall,' he said. Then, in the most matter-of-fact tone imaginable, Daddy replied, 'I have one dollar and sixty-seven cents to pay down on the supplies and I promise, by my word, I will pay you the balance within thirty days.'

"Mr. Mooreland just looked at Daddy for a few minutes without saying a word. Eventually he let out a 'What?' Daddy repeated himself. They sat across from each other for another full minute before the stock boy came by to say the car had been loaded. After that, Mr. Mooreland got up, shook Daddy's hand and okayed the deal. And just like that, we were in the pie business."

"That was it?" I asked, a little dumbstruck. It was inconceivable to me that a person could do so much with so little money, but I supposed Paul's dad had made up for it with passion and determination.

"Just about. He bought a few things from Renner's on credit — flour and lard and the like. But Daddy started the business with a dollar-sixty-seven and nerves of steel. That's the Marshall way."

Doesn't that just make me proud as pudding to be a Marshall? I thought. But I never got a chance to say it. Bud had emerged from his quietude with a thoughtful look on his face.

"Speaking of the Marshall way," he said, "I've got some news about Waco."

He proceeded to tell us about the problems he was having with the shop. Business wasn't so terrible, but it wasn't booming either. Bud wanted to explore new territory and Ruth wanted to move closer to her mother.

"We're closing down the shop in Waco and moving everything to Tulsa," he said.

I could see Paul's disappointment when his brother mentioned the city we'd been dreaming of since we started putting money aside. The family policy was that unclaimed territory was first come, first serve. We were going to lose Tulsa to Bud and Ruth because we had delayed taking it so we could save for the baby.

Suddenly, Paul perked up.

"What's gonna happen to the business in Waco, Bud?" he asked.

"I'm going to walk away and leave it."

Paul looked at me and something unspoken passed between us. It wouldn't be exactly what we'd planned. The timeline would be sooner than we'd bargained for and it wasn't exactly where we wanted to be. But we'd be making progress on our dreams nonetheless. I gave a little nod and felt a smile spread wide across my face.

"Bud," Paul said, "if you tell me when you're walking off Waco, I'd be happy to walk in right behind you."

Chapter Seven

By the middle of my third trimester, my cravings for good barbeque had gotten so strong, I would wake up from deep sleep with the sweet, smooth, smoky taste of slow-cooked pork on my tongue. I realized I'd been dreaming about it almost every night. I couldn't get enough! So it was no surprise to me that when I finally gave that baby in my belly what he wanted — a heaping plate of warm brisket oozing with dark, sticky sauce — he decided to come into the world and thank me for it in person.

John Weldon Marshall was born at 8:15 in the evening, just after dinner, on October fifteenth, 1936. Paul and I had been in Waco since August. The business was flourishing, and we were happy to be striking out on our own. Lelah came down to help me with Johnny in those first weeks, and the shop was only without me for a few days. By the beginning of 1937, we'd increased our sales by fifty percent. Waco hadn't been exactly what we wanted when we got it, but me and Paul had made it work. Waco had become the place where everything we'd been working toward had come together: our home, our business, and our family.

So when Big Daddy showed up in the middle of January to tell us that Bud and Ruth had heard about our success and wanted Waco back, Paul and I had to give the matter some serious consideration. Instantly, Paul asked the question I'd just been formulating in my mind: "Are there problems with the business we should know about?"

Big Daddy explained that Tulsa had just weathered the coldest winter in its history, and as a consequence heating expenses and truck repair costs had been unusually high. The drivers were working slower in the cold, so they brought in less money. To top it all off, Ruth wanted to be closer to her family, who were still in Waco.

It didn't seem like so long ago that Paul and I had been dreaming of Tulsa. And while we'd been happy to relocate our dreams when opportunity came knocking, doing so again would be a big risk.

It was one we were willing to take.

Paul and I were like kids in a candy store, the way we pored over every detail of the move. We only had two weeks to figure out how to make the transition as seamless as possible. In the end, we decided that each shop would bake pies on Saturday night before we headed out the door. We'd have just enough time left in the weekend to traverse the necessary 350 miles without missing a day of sales on Monday. To say we were an ambitious bunch would be to severely understate the truth, but ambitious we were. Call it youth or *joie de vivre* — we had it in spades.

But all the drive and pluck in the world couldn't have made that move less nightmarish than it turned out to be! There were flat tires and deserted highways and broken trailers — and me in the passenger seat of a 1930 Model A with my beautiful baby boy cocooned in a patchwork quilt on my lap. The temperature must have been in the twenties or below. We'd run out of diapers for Johnny miles before our caravan broke down for the third time. Credit goes to Paul, of course, for his resourcefulness; he got us to Tulsa at one in the morning.

Other people — superstitious folk — might have taken our experience as a sign that the move to Tulsa was a bad idea. Not Paul, though, and certainly not me. We'd both worked too hard in our lives to put stock in much of anything but the sweat of our brows, and we sure worked up a froth in Tulsa. Just a month after taking over, we'd turned enough of a profit to pay our rent and utilities, square our bills from suppliers, and squirrel a few dollars away. It seemed like Tulsa would be everything we'd dreamed of and more. That is, until Bill Fitcher threw a big ol' wrench in our wheels.

You see, Bill had come to Paul with a proposition for how we could save money and improve our product. Soft wheat flour, a new product from General Mills, could deliver all that and more, Bill told us. Paul, whose openness to innovation was something I'd always admired, naturally put his faith in this new food technology. Paul ordered a whole truckload of the stuff for a bargain, and as our hard flour slowly dwindled, I started baking with the soft wheat.

By the end of March, our sales had begun to plummet with alarming rapidity. We couldn't keep our pies on display like we normally did — they were starting to mold. Day after day, Paul would come home with entire trays of returned pies. I'd always been proud of the way I'd run the kitchen. As a Marshall-by-marriage, my pie-making skills had been honed, not inherited, and I knew I did Bama proud. Suddenly I was overcome by self-consciousness. Ruth's pies had been good enough to nurture the routes here without a problem. Why were sales dropping within two months of my taking charge in the kitchen?

Maybe I was in denial about the fault lying with me, or maybe I'd automatically reverted to the training I'd had at the real estate office, but one thing or another made me turn to our record books. I was convinced the numbers would have the answers, even if they seemed dire. I inspected every line item from flour to fruit fillings. I combed every ledger for some kind of clue.

Seek and ye shall find.

I could imagine a hundred-watt light bulb glowing over my head as I checked and double-checked our order sheets. When Paul got home that night, I met him at the door.

"I've got something to show you!" I said. I couldn't contain my excitement.

"You found buried treasure?" he answered wearily.

"Almost. Look at this order sheet. See how much shortening we've been ordering? For the amount of pies we fry, we shouldn't need that much shortening."

"Lilah, I'm happy to see you're rooting out waste, but I don't see how this means much. You think one of the girls is stealing it?"

"No, Paul. We're using it up. *We're using too much shortening.* Don't you see? It's why we're not selling pies like we used to. That soft wheat flour is soaking up too much grease when we fry the pies. It alters the taste and makes the dough rot more quickly."

Paul was skeptical at first but the numbers never lie. We realized the soft flour was fine for baked crusts and terrible for fried pies. Paul called Bill the next day to tell him what we'd discovered. To his credit, Bill felt terrible about all the trouble his new-fangled flour had caused. He promised to replace all our remaining soft wheat with hard wheat flour.

Even though our sales started picking up again within two weeks, it took nearly the whole summer and half the fall to overcome the damage soft wheat flour had done to our market. I felt a measure of pride at having been such an essential part of our rebound, but it was devastating to have come so far only to backslide so soon out of the gate. By Thanksgiving, though, Bama was back on top in Tulsa. Us Marshalls had a lot to be grateful for.

It felt to me and Paul that we'd been working our whole lives, so nurturing our Bama business was a familiar feeling. What neither of us had done before was raise a child. Now *that* was new and different!

Johnny was a good baby. He slept through the night relatively quickly and never really fussed. He liked the nonsense songs Paul would sing while he fed or changed him. I'd prop Johnny on my lap in front of a mirror for his favorite game: self-admiration. His rosy plump cheeks and sweet, laid-back demeanor fit in perfectly around the shop. All the ladies who worked with me in the kitchen loved him like one of their own, and the route men took the cautious interest all men take in babies that aren't their own.

Yes, Johnny was as good a baby as we could have hoped for, and Paul and I were doing our best to be fantastic parents to our son. But learning to be a parent is a lot different than learning how to bake a pie or run a business. No path is filled with more uncertainty and self-consciousness than the one traveled by a new mother and father — a truth Paul and I learned one particularly hot summer autumn in 1938.

Johnny was toddling. Any seasoned parent will tell you that once babies find their feet, yours will never be still again. Johnny was always on the move. Even the stifling heat we'd been experiencing that week didn't seem to slow him down, though all around us people looked like they were moving through molasses. The humidity stuck to your skin like glue. It was terrible!

Paul and I were closing up shop late in the afternoon. We'd sent the crew home early. The kitchens were so unbearably hot, it seemed cruel to keep anyone a moment longer than necessary. I was working the books in the back office while Paul finished the day's routine in the kitchen. I could hear the rhythmic slosh and wipe of a mop moving in and out of a bucket, then across the floor. The heat was pressing in on me from all sides and it made me more sleepy than uncomfortable. I could feel my eyelids getting heavy...

The clatter of the wooden mop handle against the floor jolted me from my hazy trance.

"Lilah!" Paul yelled.

"What is it, Paul?" I answered, but I had already started moving toward him. The panic in his voice was something I'd never heard before.

"Lilah, something's happened. Something's happened to Johnny!" Paul said. "I had him in sight all this time, and I just turned my back for a second!"

My heart leapt into my throat. I felt my senses kick into overdrive. Did I smell smoke or fire? Did I hear screaming or crying? Did I see anything unusual?

As they so often do, the eyes had it. I followed Paul's outstretched finger to a red smear low on the white wall. I raced around the kitchen, following the trail of dark smudges that seemed to be getting thicker and more erratic. I was calling Johnny's name again and again, and I could feel tears stinging the back of my eyes. As I rounded the corner on one of our big stainless steel work tables, I finally found him. Elbow-deep in an oversized tub of cherry pie filling.

To say Paul and I were overcome by joy that our baby was safe, whole, and happier than ever before would be another understatement. We both exhaled for what seemed like days, and our breathing turned to laughter. My laughter turned to tears. Paul wrapped me in his arms and we both sat on the floor next to Johnny. We even joined him in the cherry finger-painting fun. After believing — even for just an instant — that we were about to face tragedy, sour cherries tasted sweet as honey.

Chapter Eight

"I've got an idea."

Having spent as much time as I had with Paul Marshall, I knew that he'd carry around an idea like a dog with a meaty bone. It was never a matter of *if* we'd act on his ideas, only a matter of when.

"Is that right? What's this idea you've got?" I asked without looking up from the account ledger I was reviewing.

"I think we should take a trip."

That got my attention. This didn't sound like a quick run to Big Mother's house or a Sunday drive to Grace and Melvin's. Paul and I were worker bees, as you may have gathered. Travel for leisure wasn't really part of our lifestyle, especially not with John in tow. Still, I was eager to know what exotic location could have enticed my husband to make such a suggestion.

"Where would this trip take us?"

"Lawton, Oklahoma," he said. Paul's enthusiasm made the place sound irresistible, but I'll admit to being slightly disheartened. "Or

Lawton approximately, I should say."

"Lawton?"

"The Holy City of the Wichitas. We heard that broadcast last year—"

"Of the Easter Pageant! Oh, I remember, Paul. The president sent a telegram and everything!"

"Exactly! I figure, if Mr. Roosevelt took the time to send his regards, we might as well make the trip. I thought we could do it up right: drop Johnny off with my parents, stay overnight, then get an early start for the sunrise service on Easter Sunday."

"Why, that sounds wonderful, Paul!"

We made our plans for April. We set out for Big Mother and Big Daddy's house late one Saturday afternoon after preparing the shop for the following Monday's deliveries. Paul and I loaded ourselves into the car in the wee hours that night so we could get up well before dawn and make it to the Holy City in time.

Lawton's Easter Pageants had been around for almost as long as I could remember. They were staged on a stretch of land that supposedly replicated the Holy Land, and followers of Reverend Anthony Mark Wallock had built the place up like a biblical Renaissance fair. Paul and I had heard about the Holy City pageants just like everyone else, and of course we'd tuned in to listen when the passion play was broadcast over the radio in 1936. We knew a hundred thousand people had shown up that year, though it was difficult to actually conceive of that many bodies in one place. People said flowers dropped from the sky during the Resurrection scenes and skywriters zoomed through the air depicting messages of faith. In short, the pageant promised to be a spectacle like none we'd ever seen.

We knew we were close when we saw Knights Templars directing traffic. Their stark white tunics painted with red crosses stood out against the lush green countryside. Low stone walls that led to the gateways of Jerusalem sprawled on either side of the dirt roads. On foot with the other pilgrims, we walked past the Calvary Mount and the Temple Court, Pilate's Judgment Hall and the Watch Towers, the Garden of Gethsemane, and, of course, the manger in Bethlehem. Who-knows-how-many of us sat on blankets and tarps on a hillside, watching the play unfold. At sunrise, we watched the Resurrection. Sure enough, biplanes buzzing overhead dropped white flowers from their cockpits. "Christ Arose" was scrawled across the sky in wisps of white cloud. The entire mountainside was alive with the kind of joy you only ever feel when people talk about miracles on Christmas Eve, and me and Paul were as caught up as anyone.

After the play, Paul took my hand and we walked around the vast property. Eventually we sat by a small outcropping of stones near a lake. I still remember the sound of a soft breeze rippling the water against the shore. A chorus of crickets chirped their early morning song.

"Peaceful, isn't it?" Paul said. He sure had a habit of taking words right out of my mouth.

"Mmm," I replied drowsily.

"You know I've been thinking?"

"Oh?"

"It's just that Mother and Dad have done so much for us kids, helping us set up our own businesses and making Bama such a strong company. We could really have something here, something that lasts a long time. We need to keep ourselves focused on creating something really extraordinary so we can do for our children what Mother and Daddy have done for us."

"That's a beautiful thought, Paul."

We sat there letting the idea of a Marshall legacy bloom in the silence we shared. I could imagine our future together stretching out a million miles in every direction, like ripples moving away from a boulder thrown into the ocean. At the center were Big Mother and Big Daddy, and the first concentric ring was made up of all the Marshall kids and their spouses. Johnny was in the next ring. Sure, he was little then, but we knew chances were good he'd follow in Paul's footsteps in some capacity. From there, who knew? I liked that Paul had a vision that reached beyond the stretches of my imagination. He'd always been a dreamer, and I knew places like the Holy City were meant to inspire dreamers. There's something about a place that reaches back in time that makes you want to look toward the future.

Little did Paul or I know that our future at Bama would eventually be threatened by an adversary we'd never seen coming.

Through the late thirties and early forties, Paul and I worked hard to improve and grow the business. We'd embraced new technology, absorbed other bakeries into Bama, and expanded our offerings to include the sweet rolls and doughnuts that had been a specialty of Tulsa Pastry before we bought the company. We were on track to expand even further near the end of 1945, but in November, an unexpected cog was thrown in our well-oiled wheels.

A route man of ours, Randall, had gotten bit by the union bug. Our shop had never been union, though we offered a fair wage to the ladies in the kitchen and our drivers worked on a ten percent commission. When Randall tried to organize our drivers to force us into becoming a union establishment, Paul fired him. The very next day, I came into work to find a picket line marching out front. I managed to get them to disperse so our drivers could make their deliveries, but only once I agreed to have Paul meet with the union representative later that day.

From that meeting onward, things went from bad to worse. Our drivers were threatened. One was even beat up while making a delivery to the same café in Tulsa where Paul had proposed to me. Union men threw stink bombs in our trucks, destroying our products and our property. Others would smash our pies whenever they saw them in a store or restaurant. Some of our vendors whose shops were unionized refused to set foot on Bama property. The result was more work for me and Paul and those loyal employees who had decided to stay on.

Things came to a head when Paul started getting phone calls at all hours of the night. Anonymous men would call and threaten him. Paul thought I didn't know. He'd just say, "Wrong number," and pretend to go back to sleep. I knew the calls disturbed him, that he'd lie awake for hours afterward questioning why all of this was happening to us. On one such night, I decided I couldn't let Paul bear the burden of all those thoughts alone. The truth is, I had come to know a thing or two about being harassed by the union.

"Who was on the phone, Paul?" I asked.

"Wrong number," he said.

"That wasn't really a wrong number, was it?"

"What makes you think that?"

"A man called me two days ago when you were out making deliveries. I didn't say anything because I didn't want you to worry. Here you are, doing the same thing."

"What did he say?" Paul asked.

"He asked me how I'd be able to provide for Johnny if he didn't have a daddy." I could feel tears jumping to the corners of my eyes like they did each time I relived that terrible conversation.

"Anything else?" Paul was keeping the emotion from his face, but I could hear it in his voice.

"He asked if Johnny'd ever gotten lost walking home from the school bus stop. Then he asked if I knew what a broken arm felt like. Paul, I'm so scared, but I want you to know I'm ready to fight those guys. Now more than ever."

"That's my girl," he said, squeezing my hand.

That night we stayed up talking for over an hour. It was good to share our fears and our anger, and especially our disbelief. We'd been running a fair and equitable shop. As folks who'd grown up working hard, we wanted to provide a good job to those who wanted to work hard alongside us.

Picketers walked in front of our Sweet Shop for thirteen months. They wore signs that read "This Firm On Strike." They would bother our customers and our drivers all day long. Paul was talking to his friend, Red, one night about what he could do to stop the picketing. They came up with a scheme – and I still can't believe to this day what they did. Early one Sunday morning, when the picketers were nowhere in sight, Paul and Red set up a track on top of the Sweet Shop, like a train track. We dressed up a life-sized mannequin in one of Paul's fine suits, and even put a brand new Stetson cowboy hat on him. Paul and Red rigged him up so that he would go along the track – it looked like he was walking the same steps as the picketers, just above them. The last, and most important piece of the equation was the American flag that Paul rested on the mannequin's shoulder. Paul wanted the mannequin to represent the fact that the union was trying to take away our American freedoms.

Before we had even finished putting up the mannequin, drivers on Eleventh Street, which was also a part of Route 66, were stopping to take photos of our picketing dummy. Paul decided he looked too nice to be called a dummy, so we began to call him Duke. Duke became a sort of phenomenon, as reporters came from LOOK magazine, Time magazine, and even Life Magazine to get snapshots of him doing his "walk" above the picket line. A few months after Duke had been manning his post, Paul drove up to the shop to see some kids teasing the picketer who was protesting. They couldn't seem to decide who was the dummy, Duke or the man picketing. Not long after that the picketing stopped, and Duke had done his job. Paul was so proud of Duke that he kept him in the corner of his office, watching over any potential rabble-rousing that might occur.

Like those of any bully, the union's harassment tactics changed over time. When Bama and her employees were unflappable in the face of physical violence, the union would find a way to destroy our products. When we still managed to supply our buyers, the union made sure our building applications were lost and our expansions delayed. Time and again the union proved resourceful and creative, but time and again Bama proved indefatigable. It was years before the picketing stopped, and even longer before the union gave up on forcing Bama's hand. Though the threat from the unions never really changed, the pie industry did. Eventually, as our business sold more and more to supermarkets and less to small grocery stores, restaurants, and hotels, the union's influence petered out.

I still believe that the stress of that time aged Paul in a way that working hard never had. Through it all, we kept the dream of a Marshall legacy alive in our hearts. Fighting the good fight, even in the face of an enemy whose practices were underhanded and dishonest, was the only way to make our dream a reality.

Chapter Nine

About fifteen years after I become a mother for the first time, Paul and I had the great pleasure of welcoming our second son, Roger, into the world. I suppose the joy of a new baby after all that time was so overwhelming, we wanted to keep the happiness coming. Paula was born the following year, in 1953. That year also marked another important milestone in Bama's history: it was the year Paul got into the frozen pie business. It would be almost another decade before we formulated the frozen turnovers that would solidify our market hold with companies like McDonald's, but freezing our eight-inch pies was the first step.

Sadly, the decade that had started with so much new life and so much promise found its counterpoint in 1955, when Big Daddy broke his hip in a bad fall and Big Mother passed away. I felt a deep, unspeakable sadness when my mother-in-law died. She had been as close to me as my own mother, and she was the cornerstone of the Marshall clan. It was difficult for Paul too, of course, and the sight of his father's reduced mobility and listlessness didn't ease his heartache any. In November 1958, when Big Daddy passed on, our grief was appeased just knowing he'd be meeting up with Mother on the other side. Still, Paul and I spent a lot of time reflecting on how inspirational Henry and Cornelia "Alabama" Marshall had been. We knew we owed it to both of them to see Bama through to the next generation and curate the business for our children as it had been for us.

That aim was far easier said than done. The Dallas and Houston plants had closed; Bud and Ruth were hanging on by a thread in Waco. Paul's sister had sold the Memphis plant to us, and Paul had sold it to a pie man from Indiana who the unions had put out of business. Ruby was struggling in Shreveport. Two Alabama plants were forced to close, and while Grace had been plenty successful in Oklahoma City, she'd finally decided to retire from the business altogether. We were still doing fine in Tulsa, but Paul and I knew we had to keep looking to the future if we wanted to increase our profit margins and keep Bama alive.

Time marched on despite the family's personal and professional losses. The sixties brought growth and change on the large and small scales. While the Civil Rights Movement and draft protests fueled the nation's passions countrywide, Paul engineered a relationship with the McDonald's corporation that would change the course of Bama's future. Beginning in 1963, Paul traveled back and forth from Tulsa to Chicago once a week to work with McDonald's in developing a personal fried pie to add to their menu. Three years later, our product launched nationally. McDonald's helped us secure a quarter of a million dollars from our bank to expand the plant to accommodate the new demand. For perhaps the first time, Paul and I had the monetary backing to match our enthusiasm for Bama's growth. Through the research and development phases, false starts, and long trips back to the drawing board, Paul always kept his eye on the prize: building the Marshall legacy.

The McDonald's account brought enormous changes to our lives. As you might imagine, a customer with a practically endless need for our product brought a new level of prosperity to Bama. Suddenly, Paul and I had the means to spoil our family a bit, and even indulge a little ourselves. We took up golf together. Whether that particular pastime is good or bad for high blood pressure, I really can't say, but we enjoyed ourselves nonetheless.

We both still went to work every day. The business was our baby, after all, and you don't just stop being a parent once your child learns to stand on its own two feet. I spent my days in the plant until the afternoon, when I'd go pick up Roger and Paula at school. I managed to have a little fun, too — shopping at Miss Jackson's in Utica Square, trying out new spa treatments, and expanding my collection of what Paula affectionately came to call my "church lady hats."

Paul and I traveled to Holland and Japan to help set up pie plants for McDonald's. Again and again we marveled that the company Paul's mom and dad had started out of their kitchen had grown enough to bring us across the globe. We were so fortunate to have the opportunity to travel, and we never lost sight of where those opportunities originated. Even the luckiest of us has to take the sour with the sweet, though, as Paul and I had learned again and again. In 1972, we were reminded of the truth of that maxim, when Johnny had a heart attack at the age of thirty-five.

A quadruple bypass surgery saved our boy's life, but he would have to be wary of stress and high blood pressure. The diagnosis was an especially hard blow since it meant Johnny wouldn't be cut out to take over Bama when Paul was ready to retire. Paul wasn't even sixty yet, but the image of his oldest son taking up the mantle had been with him for so long, it was hard to imagine a future that didn't include its realization.

The compulsion to find a successor for Bama became even more fevered the following year, when Paul went to Atlantic City for a packaging trade show. Paul told me he was lying in bed in his hotel when he suddenly felt he couldn't breathe. Alone and desperate, he'd stuck his head out the window and gulped air until the feeling passed, but the experience spooked him. I was scared, too. The doctors told us Paul had high blood pressure and ordered us on a two-week vacation. Over his protests about not being able to leave the company, I booked us a trip to Acapulco.

Mexico really was just what the doctor ordered. For the first time, Paul and I sat back and observed that age had crept up on us like a thief in the night. Though we felt young in mind and heart, it was impossible to deny how relieved our bodies felt in the warm sun. It wasn't until we'd been in Acapulco for a few days that we even realized how much stress we were carrying around back in Oklahoma. Paul likened the sensation to taking off a pair of trousers you didn't realize were too tight until you removed them. I thought the analogy was alarmingly accurate!

Someone from the hotel recommended that we make time to watch the La Quebrada cliff divers while we were in town. Intrigued by the idea of watching such an exotic, exhilarating feat, we made our way to a restaurant with a view of the cliffs and settled in for a good show. We weren't disappointed. Divers fly through the air from 125 feet up, ultimately splashing into a narrow gulch below. The water they aim for is shallow — sometimes only a dozen feet deep — and the divers risk life and limb to make the jump time and again. I was impressed by the thrilling dives, but I noticed Paul got quiet as we watched one man after another heave himself over the edge of the cliff.

"What is it, Paul?" I asked, covering his hand with mine.

"Something about those divers, Lilah. I feel for them. They climb that mountain, say their prayers, and then leap into the unknown. Are we really so different?"

"How do you mean?"

"My parents started the Bama companies in 1927. Since then, I've been climbing the mountain, surveying the view from the top, then jumping into the future. You've done it, too. That's what it takes to build an empire and leave a legacy like we've always dreamed. I guess it's just that sitting here, watching those men dive, I got to thinking I'm feeling a little tired of the unknown."

I knew exactly what he meant. Paul and I had always been ready to take risks for our business; that was one of the passions we shared. But a lifetime of hard work was starting to tucker us out. And now, with no clear replacement for Paul at the helm of the company and his health dependent on reduced stress, uncertainty loomed once more.

We vowed to take it easy when we got back to the States, but it was hard to resist the pull of our old routines. Within a year, Paul suffered his first heart attack. We knew we had to make a change.

It was no surprise to me — though it may have been a shock to the male-dominated industry leaders we worked with — that it was Paula who ultimately stepped up to fill her father's role at Bama. Paula had worked in every possible capacity at Bama, from the pie-making floor to the accounting department to sales. She had spearheaded Bama's adoption of computers — no easy task, considering how new that technology was at the time — and was an incredibly adept mediator. She was the obvious choice to carry on the Marshall name in the Bama system. At least, it was obvious to me.

Paul was hesitant to let his little girl take the reins. It wasn't that he didn't think she was capable. We'd raised all our children to be more than capable businesspeople. It was more that Paul wanted to protect his only daughter from the burdens of bearing such a heavy load. Paula and I knew she was more than strong enough to shoulder all of Bama. Finally, in 1983, when our long-time plant manager retired, I spoke up.

"Paula can take over the shop," I said in response to Paul's musings about who could ever replace our manager.

"How do you figure? She's all right in the computer room and in sales, but since when is she qualified to run the plant?"

"I've been encouraging her for several years now to learn every phase of the business. And for the last two years, she's taken a particular interest in plant operations. She knows more about the shop than anyone. Hadn't you noticed?"

Paul was quiet, but I knew there was a light bulb glaring over his head. He'd gotten so used to seeing Paula as his little girl, he'd failed to notice she'd become a force to be reckoned with at Bama. For all the time I spent on the line making pies or working our books, I often think that five-minute conversation between me and Paul was the most important contribution I made to Bama. See, that conversation solidified our dream for a Marshall legacy — and ensured my daughter would get the dues at Bama she justly deserved.

Paul and I were freer to travel once the 1980s arrived. We'd started spending six months of the year at our condo in Naples, and we were able to travel to Europe, Canada, Rio, Panama, Costa Rica, and

Guatemala to set up pie plants for McDonald's. Every new place we journeyed to made me and Paul marvel at the incredible doors our pies had opened for us. And because we went everywhere together, it was impossible to forget that the most important door Bama had helped us find was the one that led to each other.

The girls said they wanted to hear my story. Well, I think I've relayed it as faithfully as anyone could.

We lost Paul in 1993. To say that I miss him is almost redundant, but there it is. I miss him terribly. It was with Paul by my side that I had all my greatest adventures. Loving him was the greatest by far. We grew up together, grew old together, and grew a business together. We nurtured each other, our family, and Bama. Through thick and thin, we could rely on one another, and that was always enough.

In some ways, I can appreciate now more than ever that Paul and I had a sweet, sweet life together. It's the taste of sour that sets off sweet, after all, and there's no sour quite like losing the man you love. But without the contrast, you'll never learn to taste the full depth of flavor a pie has to offer.

Life is kind of like that, if you know what I mean.

CPSIA information can be obtained at www.ICGtesting.com
Printed in the USA
LVOW040153010212

266467LV00006B/3/P